A Comparison of Vegetation Sampling Methods in Coastal Dune Scrub at Point Reyes National Seashore

Natural Resource Technical Report NPS/SFAN/NRTR—2011/516

Robert Steers, Heather Spaulding, and Eric Wrubel

National Park Service
Inventory & Monitoring
San Francisco Area Network
Ft Cronkhite Bldg 1063
Sausalito, CA 94965

December 2011

U.S. Department of the Interior
National Park Service
Natural Resource Stewardship and Science
Fort Collins, Colorado

The National Park Service, Natural Resource Stewardship and Science office in Fort Collins, Colorado publishes a range of reports that address natural resource topics of interest and applicability to a broad audience in the National Park Service and others in natural resource management, including scientists, conservation and environmental constituencies, and the public.

The Natural Resource Technical Report Series is used to disseminate results of scientific studies in the physical, biological, and social sciences for both the advancement of science and the achievement of the National Park Service mission. The series provides contributors with a forum for displaying comprehensive data that are often deleted from journals because of page limitations.

All manuscripts in the series receive the appropriate level of peer review to ensure that the information is scientifically credible, technically accurate, appropriately written for the intended audience, and designed and published in a professional manner.

This report received informal peer review by subject-matter experts who were not directly involved in the collection, analysis, or reporting of the data.

Views, statements, findings, conclusions, recommendations, and data in this report do not necessarily reflect views and policies of the National Park Service, U.S. Department of the Interior. Mention of trade names or commercial products does not constitute endorsement or recommendation for use by the U.S. Government.

This report is available from the San Francisco Bay Area Network Inventory & Monitoring program website (http://www.sfnps.org/) and the Natural Resource Publications Management website (http://www.nature.nps.gov/publications/nrpm/).

Please cite this publication as:

Steers, R. J., H. L. Spaulding, and E. C. Wrubel. 2011. A comparison of vegetation sampling methods in coastal dune scrub at Point Reyes National Seashore. Natural Resource Technical Report NPS/SFAN/NRTR—2011/516. National Park Service, Fort Collins, Colorado.

NPS 612/112015, December 2011

Contents

Figures

Tables

Appendices

Abstract

Four vegetation sampling schemes were implemented in a coastal dune scrub community that either utilized: 1) 100 m point-line intercepts, 2) 12 m point-line intercepts, 3) 10 m point-line intercepts, or 4) 10 m line intercepts. The purpose of this study was to compare the four methods in their ability to measure the cover of shrub species and species richness. When evaluating shrub cover by species, none of the four methods differed significantly. When evaluating species richness, the 100 m transect method detected higher total species richness (all species combined), herbaceous perennial species richness, and annual species richness compared to the other two point-line intercept methods. Also, the 12 m point-line intercept method recorded higher herbaceous perennial species richness than the 10 m point-line intercept. No difference in shrub species richness was found between the four methods. Lastly, data variability was the lowest and second lowest for the 100 m point-line intercept and the 12 m point-line intercept, respectively. Power analyses revealed that the 100 m point-line intercept required the least number of sample units to detect significant differences. However, if outliers are removed from the other three methods, then power analyses reveal that they require close to the same number of sample units as the 100 m point-line intercept.

Acknowledgments

Danny Lynch assisted with field sampling. Marie Denn, Lorraine Parsons, and Greg Kudray provided useful comments and suggestions to improve the manuscript. Marie Denn, Alison Forrestel, Sue Fritzke, Brent Johnson, Lorraine Parsons, and Fernando Villalba provided input on sample design.

Introduction

Effective vegetation monitoring programs utilize techniques that are time efficient, accurate, and unbiased. Improvements in time efficiency have the potential to increase the number of sample units across the study area, thus improving status while greater accuracy can improve trend detection. In addition, vegetation sampling methods that reduce opportunities for observer bias also improve trend detection. Because many national park units with vegetation monitoring programs are reliant on seasonal field crews with high inter-annual turnover, the ability to design vegetation monitoring techniques that are efficient, accurate, and unbiased have great utility.

The purpose of this study was to compare the ability of four line transect sampling methods to estimate plant cover and species richness. The methods chosen for this study compare a 100 m point-line intercept technique, which we consider to be a superior method for sampling cover in patchy, open vegetation based on personal experience, with three other methods that each utilize three shorter (10 to 12 m), radiating transects per sample. A stand of vegetation that exhibits a closed canopy and has low numbers of shrub species, typical of some chaparral vegetation types, for example, is not especially useful for comparing sampling methods since variability is low and diverse approaches to estimate cover or species richness produce similar values (see Heady et al. 1959). Instead, comparing methods in vegetation types with low or patchy plant cover, and with high species richness, are more likely to produce divergent estimations of cover and richness due to the high variability inherent of the vegetation. Thus, coastal dune vegetation was chosen for this exercise since it exhibits an open canopy and is composed of relatively numerous shrub species.

Coastal dune vegetation is characterized by a distinct flora, some with special adaptations to high levels of wind, aerosols, soil salinity, and inundation by salt water and/or sand. However, not all portions of a coastal dune complex are influenced to the same degree by wind, salt, and other environmental factors. Thus, in most dune systems and specifically in California, vegetation and dune morphology create visually distinct zones, such as the beach, nearshore dunes (foredunes), moving dunes, and backdunes (Pickart and Barbour 2007). For example, even within the beach and foredune community, salt exposure can differ greatly, which corresponds to changes in species distributions (Barbour 1978). The relatively harsh environment that is associated with dune systems translates into vegetation communities that exhibit low perennial plant cover with a high amount of interstitial space. Overall, environmental gradients are steepest from the beach towards inland portions of a dune system and vegetation reaches its highest cover in backdunes, but even these areas can exhibit low cover compared to coastal scrub or chaparral, which typically form closed canopies (Holland and Keil 1995).

Methods

The study area was located in Point Reyes National Seashore, Marin County, California, in a dune system found north of and adjacent to Abbotts Lagoon (Figure 1). The dunes in this area and throughout the outer Point Reyes Peninsula are oriented from the northwest to the southeast, following the predominant wind direction. Coastal dune scrub indicative of backdune habitat was targeted and one stand of vegetation on a southwest facing slope was chosen for sampling since it exhibited lower cover with more patchy clusters of shrubs versus the backdune scrub found primarily on opposite, northeast aspects.

Figure 1. Aerial photograph of study area with the coastal dune scrub stand that was sampled by the four different methods outlined in red.

In the selected stand, four different vegetation sampling designs were implemented to capture shrub cover. The first design consisted of placing six parallel 100 m line transects, each at least 12 m apart from each other, oriented parallel with the contour of the slope, and randomly placed throughout the hillside (Figure 2). Vegetation was sampled along each 100 m line using the point-line intercept method (Heady et al. 1959) where at every 25 cm mark along the line, all vascular plants that were in the path of a 1.6 mm steel pin, dropped vertically from each mark were recorded. The percent cover of each species was then calculated based on the total number of hits it received divided by the total number of points or marks along the line where the steel pin was dropped, in this case 400 points, then multiplied by 100.

The other three sampling designs were based on using circular plots with three transects radiating out from the center of each plot. Six 17.95 m circular plots were randomly placed throughout the stand. A stratified random sampling design that split the stand into six equal sections and placed one unit randomly in each section was utilized (Barbour et al. 1998). Within each plot, line transects that radiated out from the center of the circular plot were laid out along the top of the vegetation in three directions, 30, 150, and 270 degrees (Figure 2). Along each of the three transects per plot, vegetation was recorded.

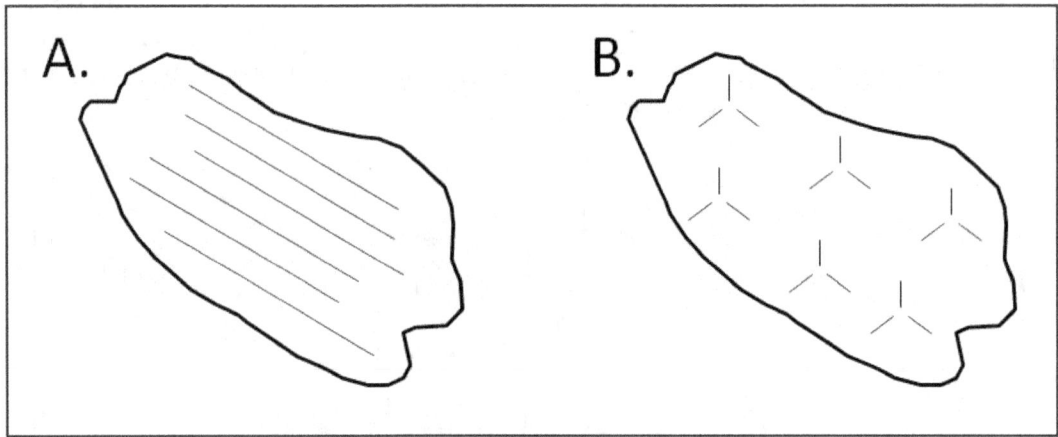

Figure 2. Depiction of the coastal dune scrub stand boundary with the six 100 m long line transects used for point-line intercept (A) and with six plots containing three radiating transects each (B), which were used for two different point-line intercept methods and one line intercept method. Figure not drawn to scale.

The first of the three methods that utilized the circular plots was a point-line intercept technique along 12 m of line, where points were taken every 25 cm from the 3.25 m mark to the 15 m mark, resulting in 48 points sampled per line. The second of these three methods, was also a point-line intercept technique where points were taken along 10 m of line every 20 cm, from the 3.20 m to the 13 m mark, resulting in 50 points per line. The percent cover of each species detected was calculated separately for both of these techniques similar to the 100 m point-line intercept method described above.

The third of the three methods that utilized the circular plots was a line intercept method (Canfield 1941). This was implemented along a 10 m segment from the 3 to the 13 m mark on each of the three lines per plot. The start and stop marks that represent the overlap of a plant species along each transect were recorded along its length. Gaps in shrub canopies were only recorded if ≥ 10 cm (Muller-Dombois and Ellenberg 1974). Cover of each plant species was calculated by dividing its total length (m) along each 10 m segment by 0.1.

All plant species were recorded by the point-line intercept technique. However, only shrub species, Aizoaceae species, and dune strawberry (Fragaria chiloensis) were recorded with the line intercept technique. Measuring all herbaceous perennials and annual plants with the line intercept technique was not possible due to time constraints (Heady et al. 1959).

Data Analyses
For comparing cover estimates between the methods, only perennial species that exhibited cover greater than one percent with all four methods were utilized in statistical analyses. The cover of each species was arcsin($\sqrt{x}$) transformed to improve normality then compared among the four

4

treatments using one-way ANOVA with a post-hoc Tukey test. Also, species richness detected by each of the techniques was also statistically compared. Since the line intercept method only sampled shrubs, Aizoaceae species, and F. chiloensis, shrub species richness could be compared among all four methods. However, for comparing total herbaceous perennial richness and annual species richness, only the three point-line intercept methods could be compared.

In addition to comparing species cover and richness among the four methods, data variability was also compared using the variable, total shrub cover, which was a composite variable based on the sum of all live cover for every shrub species detected. Total shrub cover was calculated for each of the six sample units implemented per method and then used to create box-plots that depict the sample minimum, maximum, median, lower quartile, upper quartile, and any outliers. A 95% confidence interval was also calculated using live shrub cover for each method. Because this data was non-normal based on a Shapiro-Wilk normality test ($W = 0.8109$, $P = 0.0004467$), total shrub cover was $\arcsin(\sqrt{x})$ transformed. The transformed data was then analyzed with one-way ANOVA to compare the four treatments. Also, an a priori two-tailed t-test power analysis was conducted for each of the four treatments using the transformed total live shrub cover data. The power analyses computed the required sample size to detect a 20% change in live shrub cover at 80% power and at $\alpha = 0.05$.

For all statistical analysis n = 6. For one-way ANOVAs, post-hoc tests, and summary statistics, the software, R (v.2.13.1) and the Rcmdr package were used at $\alpha = 0.05$. For power analyses the software, G*Power (v.3.1.3) was used. Lastly, cover and standard error for all species recorded during vegetation sampling are displayed based on each of the four methods utilized (Appendix A). Species nomenclature follows the Jepson Manual, 2nd Edition (Baldwin in press).

Results

Cover Estimation

The only species that were sampled by all four methods and also exhibited cover values greater than 1% were Artemisia pycnocephala, Baccharis pilularis ssp. pilularis, Carpobrotus edulis, Ericameria ericoides, Eriogonum latifolium, Fragaria chiloensis, Grindelia stricta var. platyphylla, and Lupinus chamissonis (Appendix A). Dead cover of B. pilularis ssp. pilularis and dead cover of Ericameria ericoides also exceeded one percent with all four implemented methods and were included in the comparisons. Based on the comparisons of cover values for these eight live and two dead species, no significant differences were found between the four methods (Table 1).

Table 1. Results of the one-way ANOVAs comparing cover values among the four different methods for estimating percent cover.

Species	F	P
Artemisia pycnocephala	1.0443	0.3946
Baccharis pilularis ssp. pilularis	0.3201	0.8107
B. pilularis ssp. pilularis (D)	0.0462	0.9864
Carpobrotus edulis	0.0187	0.9964
Ericameria ericoides	0.2136	0.8858
E. ericoides (D)	0.6411	0.5975
Eriogonum latifolium	0.7195	0.552
Fragaria chiloensis	0.0911	0.9641
Grindelia stricta var. platyphylla	0.0296	0.9929
Lupinus chamissonis	0.4145	0.7445

(D) indicates dead vegetation

Species Richness

Among the three point-line intercept methods utilized, the total number of species recorded differed between methods (F = 8.782, P = 0.0030). The technique that utilized 100 m long lines recorded higher numbers of species than the other two point-line intercept methods (Figure 3). When comparing all four methods in capturing shrub species richness, no differences were detected (F = 0.1543, P = 0.9257). When comparing the three point-line intercept methods at detecting numbers of herbaceous species, all three methods resulted in significantly different richness values (F = 29.137, P < 0.0001). Lastly, when comparing the three point-line intercept methods at detecting annual species richness, no differences were found (F =0.7638, P = 0.4832) (Figure 3).

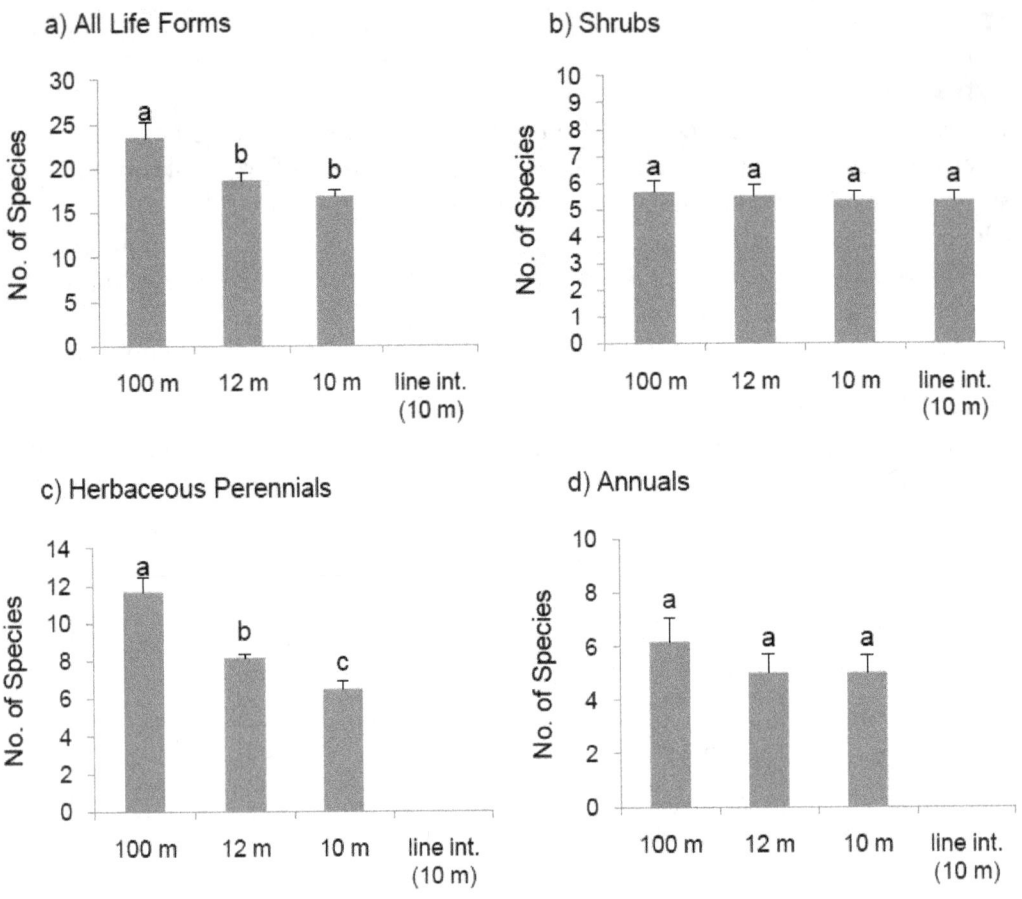

Figure 3. Comparison of the different methods at capturing numbers of unique plant species (live only) for all life forms (a), shrub species (b), herbaceous perennial species (c), and annual plant species (d). The four methods being compared are the 100 m point-line intercept (100 m), the 12 m point-line intercept (12 m), the 10 m point-line intercept (10 m), and the 10 m line intercept (line int. (10 m)), which was excluded from all comparisons except for shrub species richness.

Data Variability

When total live shrub cover was compared among the four treatments using one-way ANOVA, no statistical difference was found (F = 0.2197, P = 0.8816). However, box plots representing total live shrub cover data revealed that the 100 m point-line intercept method had the lowest spread while both of the 10 m line-based methods had the highest spread (Figure 4). 95% confidence intervals for live shrub cover were 13.7, 37.9, 49.1, and 50.4 for the 100 m point-line intercept, 12 m point-line intercept, 10 m point-line intercept, and 10 m line intercept methods, respectively.

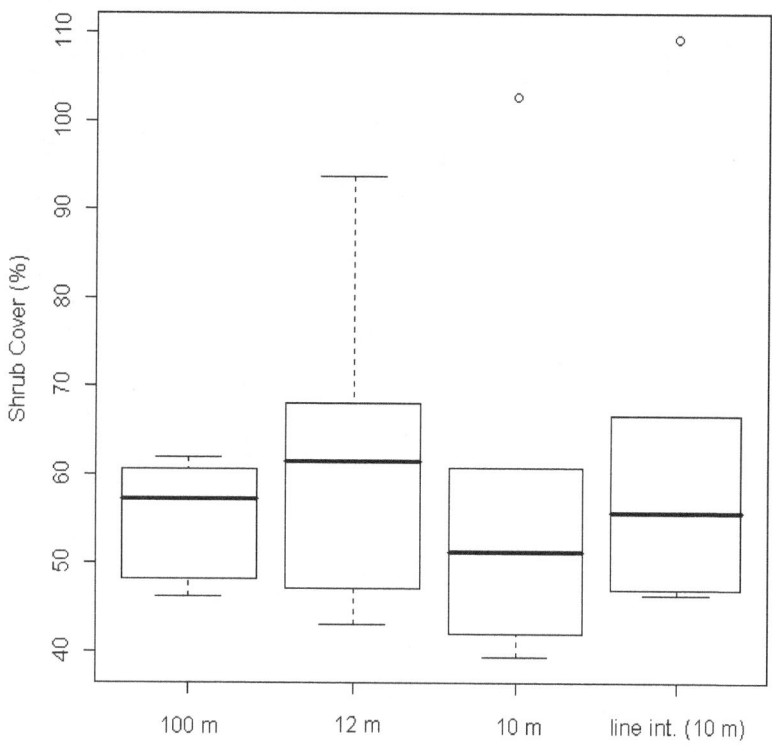

Figure 4. Boxplots of the variable, total live shrub cover, measured by 100 m point-line intercept (100 m), 12 m point-line intercept (12 m), 10 m point-line intercept (10 m), and 10 m line intercept (line int. (10 m)).

Power analyses based on two-tailed t-tests found that for the 100 m point-line intercept method a sample size of 4 was sufficient to detect a 20% change in cover at α = 0.05. To detect the same change, a sample size of 13, 29, and 24 were required for the 12 m point-line intercept, 10 m point-line intercept, and 10 m line intercept methods, respectively. However, when an outlier for the two 10 m line-based methods (Figure 4) was removed from the data set, power analyses revealed that a sample size of six, five, and five were sufficient to detect a 20% change in cover at α = 0.05 using the 12 m point-line intercept, 10 m point-line intercept, and 10 m line intercept methods, respectively.

Discussion

Cover Estimation

A diversity of techniques exists for estimating plant cover in the field. For how well-known and widely used line-based methods are, such as line intercept and point-line intercept, they have seldom been directly compared in the literature. Heady et al. (1959) compared line intercept, point-line intercept, and charting (mapping cover in the field on paper maps) and found no difference in cover estimates among those three methods in chaparral vegetation but concluded that point-line intercept was advantageous because it was the fastest. In contrast, Booth et al. (2006) compared steel point frame, laser point frame, line intercept, point-line intercept, visual estimation within a 0.1 m² quadrat, and digital images at estimating plant cover in an open-canopy sagebrush community and found point-line intercept and steel point frame to be the most accurate while line intercept was the least accurate.

The majority of literature that compares different vegetation coverage techniques does not directly compare line intercept with point-line intercept methods. Instead, line intercept and point-line intercept are separately compared with other non-line techniques. In studies examining line intercept with other non-line techniques, line intercept can be more precise than visual estimates (Hanley 1978) but can also overestimate cover compared to point quadrats and visual estimation if canopy gaps are ignored (Floyd and Anderson 1987). Also, line intercept is usually more time consuming than other approaches (Fiala et al. 2006). Lastly, orientation of line intercepts can influence accuracy. For example, many random points with short, radiating line transects per point can be more accurate than a single, long, line transect (Etchberger and Krausman 1997). In studies examining point-line intercept with other non-line techniques, point-line intercept can be similar to point quadrat (Godinez-Alvarez et al. 2009) but more accurate than visual estimates (Vittoz and Guisan 2007, Godinez-Alvarez et al. 2009, although see Symstad et al. 2008). Point-line intercept can also be faster than visual estimates (Miller et al 2006, Symstad et al. 2008).

Factors that influence comparisons among line-based techniques can include: length of transects, number of transects, size of canopy gaps included as plant cover (e.g. w/ line intercept), number and distribution of points per transect (e.g. w/ point-line intercept), orientation of transects with slope contours, patterning (radiating vs. solitary lines), and placement (non-random, random, stratified random, etc.). When comparing line-based techniques with non-line techniques, like visual estimates of cover in quadrats, the number of influences is further compounded. Not only are factors that affect line-based techniques important, but factors that influence the non-line techniques are also at play. For example, visual estimates may vary widely among observers (Cheal 2008) and can be more inaccurate when using large quadrats (i.e. 100 m²) (van Hees and Mead 2000). The number of observers, their training, other sources of observer bias, size of quadrat, shape of quadrat, number of quadrats, etc. will influence the cover estimates derived and their comparison with other methods and even between observation years.

Obviously, differences that arise among separate methodologies for estimating plant cover can be due to a number of factors. However, physiognomy is likely to be one of the most important considerations for determining which methodology is best suited for capturing structural properties. Although this study did not compare the methods in contrasting physiognomies, our results are similar to Heady et al. (1959), which was conducted in a shrubland and also found no difference in cover between line intercept and point-line intercept techniques. Based on our prior experience in shrublands, we feel line-based techniques work better than distance-based methods, quadrats using visual estimates of cover, or other non-line techniques. However, in a different physiognomy, like a forest with tall trees, line-based techniques can be inefficient and imprecise (Fiala et al. 2006). Lastly, while most studies, like ours, are often comparing techniques that have already been parameterized, usually based on prior experiences, to best capture the properties of the specific vegetation type being sampled, it is still important to mention many of the factors that can influence accuracy (Winkworth 1955, Stampfli 1991, Inouye 2002, Klimes 2003).

Species Richness

In this study, the method that utilized 100 m long line transects performed best at capturing the highest number of plant species. The two point-line intercept methods that had three, 10 or 12 m radial transects per sample unit, did not differ in number of species detected for shrub and annual life forms but did differ for herbaceous perennials, which were the most species-rich life form of all. For the later, the 12 m long transects with points recorded every 25 cm detected more herbaceous perennials than the 10 m transects with points recorded every 20 cm likely because of the greater length and wider dispersion of points. Lastly, shrub species were the only life form that could be compared among all four methods implemented but no statistical differences were found.

Although there were some differences in species richness between the methods implemented, in general, line-based techniques are relatively ill-suited for measuring species richness. Specifically, point-line intercept and a similar technique, point quadrats that rely on a steel pin being dropped along evenly spaced points within a quadrat, only record what is 'hit' by the pins, whereas visual estimates of cover for all species within quadrats detect all species per unit area. Thus, one dimensional sampling techniques (e.g. line intercept, point-line intercept, or point quadrats) typically record fewer species than visual estimates of cover within quadrats (Kercher et al. 2003, Korb et al. 2003, Symstad et al. 2008, Friedmann 2009, Godinez-Alvarez et al. 2009). Ideally, a method that records species richness per unit area and at multiple spatial scales (e.g. nested quadrats) will most likely capture the best representation of species richness, will be well suited for species-area analyses, and will be able to capture the richness of different life forms at appropriate scales; however, performance will depend on size, shape, orientation, and number of nested quadrats (Critchley and Poulton 1998, Stohlgren et al. 1998, Barnett and Stohlgren 2003, Keeley and Fotheringham 2005).

Data Variability

Among the four methods utilized in this study, data derived with the 100 m point-line intercept method had the smallest spread, the tightest confidence interval, and required the smallest sample size to detect a ± 20% change in cover. This superior performance was expected and is why the 100 m point-line intercept was chosen for this study. The next best method in terms of data variability was the 12 m point-line intercept. Although the spread of the data was similar to the other two radial, line-based methods, it had a much smaller confidence interval and required less than half the sample units needed to measure a ± 20% change in cover. Lastly, the two radial methods that utilized 10 m lines were fairly equal in terms of data spread, confidence interval, and results from the power analyses. Interestingly, once the outlier plot was removed, they outperformed the 12 m point-line intercept based on the power analyses (required one less sample (n = 5 versus n = 6) to detect a ± 20% change in cover).

These summary statistics and power analyses demonstrate how variability can influence the utility of a data set. For within-stand analyses, similar to what was presented herein, the variability in data can have a large influence on its utility to track change over time. However, it is important to remember that mean cover for total live shrub cover and also for the eight live and two dead plant species that were compared among all four methods showed no statistical difference. Thus, when comparing coastal dune scrub stands across Point Reyes National Seashore (PRNS), or between-stand analyses, any of these four methods could perform equally well. In this case, the method chosen will not be as important as the variability found across the different stands being sampled.

Conclusions

Although the time required to implement each method was not recorded, we know from previous experiences and other studies (e.g. Heady et al. 1959) that point-line intercept is faster than line intercept, especially when multiple species have overlapping canopies, like in species rich shrublands. Also, the repeatability of measurements among different observers was not examined in this study but is very important for long-term trend detection (Symstad et al. 2008). Techniques that are simple and rely on as little subjectivity as possible will likely be less prone to observer bias or errors (although this can depend on training). In regards to repeatability, we prefer point-line intercept over line intercept because it is more straight forward, leaving less room for errors due to recording where multiple overlapping shrub canopies start or stop and how to record canopy gaps.

Based on comparisons of mean shrub cover among the four techniques, no differences were found. Based on species richness, the 100 m point-line intercept was superior overall, and the 12 m point-line intercept performed better than the 10 m point-line intercept for detecting herbaceous perennials. Based on data variability, the 100 m point-line intercept had the smallest confidence interval and required the lowest sample size to detect a 20% change in total shrub cover, as expected. Also, the 12 m point-line intercept had less data variability than the other two line-based techniques. Lastly, we found that removal of an outlier with the three radial-based methods achieved data variability that was similar to the 100 m point-line intercept. Overall, the 100 m point-line intercept technique is superior in this system for producing data with low variability and for being able to detect high numbers of species. However, if capturing shrub cover is of interest, the other three methods also gave suitable results. Furthermore, this study focused on within-stand analyses but if between-stand analyses of shrub cover are conducted, then all four methods are equally likely to work since variation will be primarily due to differences between stands.

This study was not an attempt to determine the best way to sample coastal dune scrub vegetation. Rather, it was done to determine which of the three radial-based methods performed best when compared to a more standard, proven method (i.e. 100 m point-line intercept). A shrub dominated vegetation type with relatively high species richness and an open, patchy canopy was utilized since it was believed doing so would bring-out more differences in the methods being compared rather than if a homogenous, closed canopy shrubland with low species richness was utilized. Based on the results, we feel that a radial-based method for estimating shrub cover can perform acceptably and that the 12 m point-line intercept has advantages over the other two radial-based methods.

Literature Cited

Baldwin, B. G. (ed.). *In press*. The Jepson Manual, 2nd Edition. University of California Press, Berkeley, CA. Accessed from http://ucjeps.berkeley.edu/jepsonmanual/review/index.html (accessed 3 October 2011).

Barbour, M. G. 1978. Salt spray as a microenvironmental factor in the distribution of beach plants at Point Reyes, California. Oecologia 32:213-224.

Barbour, M. G., J. H. Burk, W. D. Pitts, F. S. Gilliam, and M.W. Schwartz. 1998. Terrestrial Plant Ecology, Third Edition. Benjamin Cummings, San Francisco, CA.

Barnett, D. T. and T. J. Stohlgren. 2003. A nested-intensity design for surveying plant diversity. Biodiversity and Conservation 12:255-278.

Booth, D. T., S. E. Cox, T. W. Meikle, and C. Fitzgerald. 2006. The accuracy of ground-cover measurements. Rangeland Ecology & Management 59:179-188.

Canfield, R. H. 1941. Application of the line interception method in sampling range vegetation. Journal of Forestry 39:388- 394.

Cheal, D. 2008. Repeatability of cover estimates? Ecological Management & Restoration 9:67-68.

Cook, C. W. and T. W. Box. 1961. A comparison of the loop and point methods of analyzing vegetation. Journal of Range Management 14:22-27.

Critchley, C. N. R. and S. M. C. Poulton. 1998. A method to optimize precision and scale in grassland monitoring. Journal of Vegetation Science 9:837-846.

Etchberger, R. C. and P. R. Krausman. 1997. Evaluation of five methods for measuring desert vegetation. Wildlife Society Bulletin 25:604-609.

Fiala, A. C. S., S. L. Garman, and A. N. Gray. 2006. Comparison of five canopy cover estimation techniques in the western Oregon Cascades. Forest Ecology and Management 232:188-197.

Floyd, D. A. and J. E. Anderson. 1987. A comparison of three methods for estimating plant cover. Journal of Ecology. 75:221-228.

Friedmann, B., H. Pauli, M. Gottfried, and G. Grabherr. 2011. Suitability of methods for recording species numbers and cover in alpine long-term vegetation monitoring. Phytocoenologia 41:143-149.

Godínez-Alvarez, H., J. E. Herrick, M. Mattocks, D. Toledo, and J. Van Zee. 2009. Comparison of three vegetation monitoring methods: their relative utility for ecological assessment and monitoring. Ecological Indicators 9:1001-1008.

Hanley, T. A. 1978. A comparison of the line-interception and quadrat estimation methods of determining shrub canopy coverage. Journal of Range Management 31:60-62.

Heady, H. F., R. P. Gibbens, and R. W. Powell. 1959. A comparison of the charting, line intercept, and line point methods of sampling shrub types of vegetation. Journal of Range Management 12:180-188.

Holland, V. L. and D. J. Keil. 1995. California Vegetation. Kendall/Hunt Publishing Co, Dubuque, IA.

Inouye, R. S. 2002. Sampling effort and vegetative cover estimates in sagebrush steppe. Western North American Naturalist 62:360-364.

Keeley, J. E. and C. J. Fotheringham. 2005. Plot shape effects on plant species diversity measurements. Journal of Vegetation Science 16:249-256.

Kercher, S. M., C. B. Frieswyk, and J. B. Zedler. 2003. Effects of sampling teams and estimation methods on the assessment of plant cover. Journal of Vegetation Science 14:899-906.

Klimeš, L. 2003. Scale-dependent variation in visual estimates of grassland plant cover. Journal of Vegetation Science 14:815-821.

Korb, J. E., W. W. Covington, and P. Z. Fulé. 2003. Sampling techniques influence understory plant trajectories after restoration: an example from Ponderosa pine restoration. Restoration Ecology 11:504-515.

Miller, M. E., D. Witwicki, R. Mann. 2006. Field-based evaluations of sampling methods for long-term monitoring of upland ecosystems on the Colorado Plateau – 2005 Annual Report. U.S. Geological Survey, Southwest Biological Science Center. 223 pages.

Pickart, A. J., and M. G. Barbour. 2007. Beach and Dune. Chapter 6 in M. G. Barbour, T. Keeler-Wolf, and A. S. Schoenherr (eds.). Terrestrial Vegetation of California, 3rd Edition. University of California Press, Berkeley.

Seefeldt, S. S. and D. T. Booth. 2006. Measuring plant cover in sagebrush steppe rangelands: a comparison of methods. Environmental Management 37:703-711.

Stampfli, A. 1991. Accurate determination of vegetational change in meadows by successive point quadrat analysis. Vegetatio 96:185-194.

Stohlgren, T. J., K. A. Bull, and Y. Otsuki. 1998. Comparison of rangeland vegetation sampling techniques in the central grasslands. Journal of Range Management 51:164-172.

Symstad, A. J., C. L. Wienk, and A. D. Thorstenson. 2008. Precision, repeatability, and efficiency of two canopy-cover estimate methods in northern Great Plains vegetation. Rangeland Ecology & Management 61:419-429.

van Hees, W. W. S. and B. R. Mead. 2000. Ocular estimates of understory vegetation structure in a closed *Picea glauca/Betula papyrifera* forest. Journal of Vegetation Science 11:195-200.

Vittoz, P. and A. Guisan. 2007. How reliable is the monitoring of permanent vegetation plots? A test with multiple observers. Journal of Vegetation Science 18:413-422.

Winkworth, R. E., R. A. Perry, and C. O. Rossetti. 1962. A comparison of methods of estimating plant cover in an arid grassland community. Journal of Range Management 15:194-196.

Appendix A

Appendix A. Mean cover and standard error of all plant species obtained by four different vegetation sampling methods: 100 m point-line intercept transects where vegetation was recorded every 25 cm (100m, 25pt/m); six points with three emanating radial transects 120 degrees apart where 1) a 12 m segment on each line was used for point-line intercept every 25 cm (12m, 25pt/m), 2) a 10 m segment on each line was used for point-line intercept every 20 cm (10m, 20pt/m), and 3) a 10 m segment on each line was used for point-line intercept (10m).

Family and Species	Sampling Method			
	Point-line Intercept			Line Intercept
	100m, 25pt/m	12m, 25pt/m	10m, 20pt/m	10m
Aizoaceae				
* Carpobrotus edulis	1.00 ± 0.64	1.62 ± 1.04	2.00 ± 1.28	2.07 ± 1.33
* C. chilensis	0.46 ± 0.29	1.04 ± 0.80	0.78 ± 0.50	1.19 ± 0.90
* Tetragonia tetragonioides	0.08 ± 0.08			
Apiaceae				
Daucus pusillus	0.17 ± 0.17			
Asteraceae				
Abronia latifolia	0.04 ± 0.04	0.12 ± 0.12		
Achillea millefolium	2.46 ± 0.68	4.17 ± 1.86	3.22 ± 2.08	
Agoseris apargioides var. eastwoodiae	0.08 ± 0.08			
Artemisia pycnocephala	9.79 ± 1.30	6.83 ± 1.96	5.78 ± 1.96	8.12 ± 2.15
A. pycnocephala (D)	1.04 ± 0.10	0.69 ± 0.57	0.78 ± 0.44	0.06 ± 0.05
Baccharis pilularis ssp. pilularis	8.08 ± 3.24	9.61 ± 2.87	10.22 ± 3.01	11.36 ± 3.18
B. pilularis ssp. pilularis (D)	2.88 ± 0.85	3.36 ± 1.53	3.56 ± 1.21	3.17 ± 1.22
Ericameria ericoides	19.83 ± 3.24	28.24 ± 8.15	26.89 ± 8.12	28.09 ± 7.90
E. ericoides (D)	10.63 ± 1.96	7.76 ± 1.80	7.56 ± 2.03	7.02 ± 2.77
Erigeron glaucus	0.17 ± 0.17	0.12 ± 0.12	0.22 ± 0.22	0.12 ± 0.12
E. glaucus (D)	0.08 ± 0.08			
Gamochaeta ustulata	0.13 ± 0.13			
Grindelia stricta var. platyphylla	2.92 ± 2.09	3.24 ± 1.53	3.11 ± 1.74	4.35 ± 2.43
G. stricta var. platyphylla (D)		0.23 ± 0.23		0.23 ± 0.23
* Hypochaeris glabra	0.04 ± 0.04			
! Layia carnosa		0.12 ± 0.12		
Pseudognaphalium stramineum	0.79 ± 0.31	0.93 ± 0.43	0.56 ± 0.32	
* Sonchus asper	0.04 ± 0.04			
* S. oleraceus	0.08 ± 0.05			
Boraginaceae				
Amsinckia spectabilis var. spectabilis	0.54 ± 0.25	0.46 ± 0.23	0.33 ± 0.15	
Cryptantha leiocarpa	0.33 ± 0.18	0.46 ± 0.23	0.56 ± 0.27	
Brassicaceae				
Cardamine oligosperma var. oligosperma		0.12 ± 0.12	0.22 ± 0.22	
! Erysimum franciscanum	0.46 ± 0.10	0.12 ± 0.12	0.22 ± 0.14	
Caryophyllaceae				
Cardionema ramosissimum	0.71 ± 0.44	0.70 ± 0.69	0.78 ± 0.78	
* Stellaria media	0.04 ± 0.04			
Crassulaceae				
Crassula connata		0.23 ± 0.15	0.11 ± 0.11	
Dudleya farinosa	1.33 ± 0.70	1.51 ± 0.92	0.89 ± 0.59	1.03 ± 0.67
D. farinosa (D)	0.13 ± 0.13	0.12 ± 0.12	0.11 ± 0.11	

Family and Species	Sampling Method			
	Point-line Intercept			Line Intercept
	100m, 25pt/m	12m, 25pt/m	10m, 20pt/m	10m
Cuscutaceae				
Cuscuta californica	0.13 ± 0.13		0.11 ± 0.11	
Fabaceae				
Acmispon heermannii var. *orbicularis*	1.63 ± 1.03	1.97 ± 1.22	1.56 ± 0.86	
Lathyrus littoralis	0.29 ± 0.29	0.35 ± 0.35	0.44 ± 0.44	
Lupinus arboreus	0.92 ± 0.58	1.16 ± 1.16	1.56 ± 1.31	1.64 ± 1.52
L. arboreus (D)	0.08 ± 0.05			
L. chamissonis	12.50 ± 2.15	11.46 ± 4.51	10.22 ± 5.96	10.54 ± 6.34
L. chamissonis (D)	0.92 ± 0.58		0.44 ± 0.44	0.53 ± 0.46
Lamiaceae				
! *Monardella undulata*		0.23 ± 0.23	0.22 ± 0.22	
Onagraceae				
Camissonia cheiranthifolia ssp. *cheiranthifolia*	1.92 ± 0.36	2.08 ± 0.76	1.67 ± 0.68	
C. cheiranthifolia ssp. *cheiranthifolia* (D)			0.11 ± 0.11	
Poaceae				
Bromus carinatus	0.08 ± 0.08	0.58 ± 0.38	0.22 ± 0.14	
B. carinatus (D)	0.04 ± 0.04			
Leymus mollis ssp. *mollis*	0.83 ± 0.24	0.93 ± 0.43	0.22 ± 0.14	
L. mollis ssp. *mollis* (D)	0.58 ± 0.58	0.58 ± 0.58	0.56 ± 0.56	
Poa douglasii	1.50 ± 0.28	1.27 ± 0.73	1.11 ± 0.66	
P. douglasii (D)	0.17 ± 0.08	0.35 ± 0.35	0.44 ± 0.33	
* *Vulpia bromoides*	10.04 ± 3.46	13.54 ± 3.92	14.11 ± 4.01	
Polygonaceae				
! *Chorizanthe cuspidata* var. *cuspidata*	0.13 ± 0.06	0.12 ± 0.12	0.22 ± 0.14	
Eriogonum latifolium	3.21 ± 0.71	3.70 ± 1.07	1.89 ± 0.83	2.47 ± 1.12
E. latifolium (D)	0.67 ± 0.26	1.04 ± 0.39	0.78 ± 0.21	0.37 ± 0.19
Polygonum paronychia	0.97 ± 0.68	1.51 ± 0.92	1.33 ± 0.91	1.19 ± 0.77
Pterostegia drymarioides	16.38 ± 3.33	18.98 ± 3.56	17.89 ± 3.90	
* *Rumex acetosella*	0.38 ± 0.33	1.62 ± 1.62	1.56 ± 1.56	
Polypodiaceae				
Polypodium californicum	0.04 ± 0.04			
Portulacaceae				
Claytonia perfoliata ssp. *perfoliata*	0.21 ± 0.14	0.93 ± 0.69	0.33 ± 0.33	
Primulaceae				
* *Anagallis arvensis*	0.04 ± 0.04			
Rosaceae				
Fragaria chiloensis	2.75 ± 1.46	3.24 ± 2.97	4.11 ± 3.98	2.46 ± 2.32
F. chiloensis (D)	0.04 ± 0.04			
Rubiaceae				
Galium aparine	0.54 ± 0.21	0.93 ± 0.43	0.78 ± 0.21	
Solanaceae				
Solanum americanum	0.04 ± 0.04	0.12 ± 0.12	0.11 ± 0.11	

* Exotic plant species
(D) Dead vegetation
! Special status based on USFWS, CDFG, and/or CNPS listings

NPS 612/112015, December 2011